THE ANCESTOR: A STREET PLAY

By Gayl Jones

Characters: Woman, Poet, The old man, The young man,

The feather-dancers

Scene: An old man is sitting in the center with a barrel between his knees. There are many colored feathers on the ground beside him. Reds, blues, greens, yellows, etc. Every now and then he picks up a feather and puts it on--on his arms, in his belt, into his hair, etc. Other times he looks into the barrel. The woman comes in and stands watching him. Silence. She is dressed in many colors, colors that match the feathers. She wears bracelets and many colored beads. Again, the beads match the feathers and the colors in her garment. She may also wear a feathered headdress. She doesn't speak until the old man looks up at her.

Woman: They surrounded them and got to the top of the cliffs. Even my eyelids were bruised with wanting something better to happen than that. The white men had muskets. Surrender! Rather than surrender, our men jumped. (Pause) I began singing. The other women began singing. The men grew wings. They sprouted wings) It was like the old place, you know, the old country. Palmares. The palm forest. In the new world, Brazil, but it was like the old country. It was like our Africa. Palm trees and oil. My body rubbed in palm oil. Did I drink palm wine? We were there. We were both there. I am Zumbi's woman, the best and bravest of them. I will tell you about him. He was a strong and tender man. He was a leopard. Yes, he was a leopard. I began singing. Some will tell you he jumped and was killed. Others will tell you he went on fighting, resisting. But they all will tell you he was destroyed.

The old man: What do you say?

Woman: That I began singing. That you smiled at me,
Zumbi, and then you jumped. That you took off like a bird.
That you took off like a bird, like a bird of many feathers.
That you and the other men took off like birds. We were
singing that day. All of the women were singing. Birdsong.

The old man: You're dreaming, woman.

Woman: No, this is memory.

The old man: They had him I tell you.

Woman: No, he looked at me and smiled. I began
singing. And he turned into a bird. Or grew feathers like
one. And off he flew.

The old man: Memory plus dream equals fantasy, legend, myth. You lost your memory and replaced it with a dream. This, woman, is your dream of him.

Woman: No, I saw him flying.

The old man: What do you see in this barrel, woman?

(She looks in the barrel.)

Woman: He hurls himself into his fear and his pain and it gives him wings.

(The old man smiles.)

Woman: I am singing. You smile at me, Zumbi, and then you jump. You take off like a bird. You and the others take off like birds. Birds with lovely feathers.

   (She stands away and folds her hands across her bosom, in a gesture of love, looks at him, then exits. The old man watches her leave, then puts on more feathers. The poet enters; facing away from the old man, he recites.)

Poet: And the ancestor was walking

       And the ancestor was listening

       And the ancestor was flying

       And the ancestor was flying

       And the ancestry was a bird flying

       And the ancestor was Yardbird

And the ancestor was the heavy belly of a woman

And the ancestor as a papa, too

The ancestor was a sweet papa

The ancestor told stories that were good

For men and women, forever and forever good

The ancestor saw visions that were good

For men and women, forever and forever good.

The ancestor was old but he never grew ugly

Or crazy with age

He was like a shaman, a diviner, a healer

The ancestor saw and felt things--

That lasted forever and ever

The ancestor from the beginning

Had all of us inside his eyes.

The great ancestor, his hair as thick

As bushes,

He peeled words and made stories--

His woman was the earth, you know,

Yes she was.

Her belly is heavy with life

They gave birth to each other

And then came together and made us--

We are a continuance

Of their flesh and voices.

Do not forget them.

Do not forget their stories.

Do not forget them,

For we are also their dreams.

The ancestor drinks from rivers.

He is an old man

He is a lion.

His color like ours, comes from the earth.

He is the root of God.

(The poet turns to the old man.)

Poet: What year was it, Father?

The old man: The year one thousand six hundred and

something. I can't always remember.

Poet: What happened?

The old man: I saw my uncle shaking hands with them,

the white men. The Portuguese or was it the Dutch? After

we had fought them so long, and what did they promise?

Amnesty? Freedom without manhood. It made me angry,

after we had fought them so long, and my uncle, standing

there smiling, as if their words were magic. I said those of you who will come with me, come with me, because the

old leopards have lost their spots. They are no longer

leopards. They are something other. Some stayed, some

came with me, and we found a new place, a place with

palm trees...Palmares...Of course they came after us.

They didn't want us to be men. (He says nothing else,

puts on feathers.)

Poet: And the ancestors were birds flying

      They were winged leopards

The old man: (Not talking to the poet, putting on feathers.)

      My soul is made out of blues and blood

      Everything happens again in this world

      The gods go and come

The leoards lose their spots

And replace them with wings

The women watch their bellies swell

And become flat again

Poet: Everything happens again in this world

Those who have forgotten

The soil grows flowers remember

They pat the earth with their hands

They embrace a living woman

They hold children again

They remember that the memory too is

Made out of flesh and blood--

(breaks out of tone)

The cries of the dancers

The old man: What?

Poet: They remember that love is all that endures

They remember…

The old man: Get away. One must get away from here to

have dreams. This is no place for dreaming.

(The poet exits. The old man puts on feathers,

solemn, begins talking. The young man enters while he is

talking, and stands watching him.)

The old man: I smell an aroma

I smell an aroma of blues

Consuming my blood

An aroma of blues

I told him not to

I said please do not

Leave me here in this place

I said this place is not my home

Blues flying

And then we banded together

Banded together and then came here

Became free men again

Made our own place

This is my borned place

But my spirit flows into

And from a place I was not born

The ancestors are flying

They are ascending

The ancestors are ascending

We are clustered here

Now the women have come

And they bring love

Now we have become free men and free

women again

The young man: Old man, what are you talking about?

The old man: What do you see in this barrel?

The young man: (looks in the barrel) Nothing.

The old man: Then that's what you see. Others see

bread and sardines, if they are hungry. One man saw a

woman, because he was in need of love. What are you in

need of?

The young man: Let me look again. (He looks, shakes

his head.) I still see nothing.

The old man: Some see their history, their own and others

One woman said she saw me in here, me as a young

man. Me when my muscles were long and lean and my

flesh was like new earth. She saw me when I looked

much like you. She was my woman. And she saw herself,

big-bellied and arched in pain. And she saw the side of a

huge mountain. One man saw his freedom here and

thought he could leap to it. It did him no good. He went

insane. Certain old men and old women see the rebirth of

their memories here, their dreams. Don't ask me what I

see.

The young man: Why not? You go around asking everybody else.

The old man: Maybe what I see is only what my eyes and flesh can bear.

(The young man laughs, looks in the barrel again, lifts it, turns it over, nothing comes out, gives it back to the old man. The old man continues putting on feathers.)

The old man: But you couldn't see the bottom, could you?

The young man: No.

The old man: And it didn't bother you?

The young man: No.

The old man: One woman thought her womb was there, turned inside out. She had lost a child. She herself had been the cause of that loss. A warrior woman. You know what I mean?

The young man: Yes.

The old man: So she saw her womb here and many seeds. But after she looked in, she lost her guilt. It fell to the bottom.

The young man: I thought there was no bottom.

The old man: (smiling) For you. For others yes. For some the bottom is where the top is. For some the barrel even has a lid on.

The young man: You're just plain crazy. You're a crazy old man.

The old man: Perhaps. Some find blood and sweat here. Others find bread for their children. When they find bread, I let them reach in and get it. Some find dough, and plenty of it, and go home and bake their own bread. Knead it and mould it as they will. In whatever shape they want. They bake their sweat inside the bread. They give it their strength….Go on now. You can't even see my woman, arched in pain, giving birth to you.

The young man: No, not me. You're crazy.

The old man: Her belly is covered with scars, my woman.
All of her children are of one flesh and blood, but
sometimes they can't even see each other. One feeling
flows through them, but sometimes they are afraid to know
this. The skin on her belly is scared and broken, my
woman, from bearing so many. The skin on her belly has
scabs, sometimes, but sometimes it is as whole as a
drum, a steel one. Her laughter cracks with pain, when
she laughs, and most of her children, the young ones like
you, can't see her. She is not whole; she has no bottom,
no beginning. But she is a whole woman, a whole
big-bellied woman, her breasts are cups, loaves of bread
full of milk and love. Her arms are always open and ready
to receive you.

The young man: Leave me alone.

The old man: What have I done? I'm a truth teller. I've merely told you the truth. Go on then. They have suckled her breasts and do not remember.

The young man: Shit. Enough of your nonsense. (exits)

The old man: When the white men--were they Dutch or Portuguese?--came upon us, we were at the edge of the cliff. They surrounded us. They thought they had us, that they had captured us, but when they got close, we turned and lept from the cliff. They expected us to land on the ground or in the water. But we took to the air, like birds, and were flying. (looks in the barrel) See, your ancestors are flying. There are men here. There are women here.

Even our children.

(The old man turns the barrel over and it becomes a

drum. He begins beating it to his poem, and then when

the feather-dancers enter, he continues beating the drum

and starts to chant.)

Woman, I will not let your breasts wither

Woman, I will return to you

I will not let your breasts wither

Woman, our embrace will heal the scars

In your womb

It will heal the scars

Did you come to me again

Full of elbows and laughter

Full of elbows?

You have done with your ceremony

Of waiting

You have done with your ceremony

Of waiting

I have returned

I have returned

Riding the air

Who are all of you who want

The juice from a woman's womb

And not the blood?

I said I have returned

I have returned

Riding the air

They thought we would jump to our deaths, but we sprouted

Wings, and took to the air like birds.

(The feather dancers, all men, enter. When their

dance ends, this is the culmination of the ritual.)*

*This ritual play involves the legend of Palmares, a

settlement made up of escaped or fugitive slaves in Brazil

in the 17th century. Fourteen times the whites--first the

Dutch and then the Portugues--tried to destroy the

settlement. Finally, however, they did, and the men,

cornered on a cliff, rather than surrender, jumped. The

metaphor here, however, is that rather than jumping to

their deaths they sprouted wings, became birds, and flew

away. And in this act of jumping, they retain their

manhood, their "soul". In the dance ritual, and

choreography, all of this should be clear.